The Christ Cycle
in Verse and 3D

The Christ Cycle in Verse and 3D

Reflections as Stations of the Life and Legacy of Christ in Verse and Sculpture

TODDY HOARE

Foreword by Peter Sedgwick

RESOURCE *Publications* · Eugene, Oregon

THE CHRIST CYCLE IN VERSE AND 3D
Reflections as Stations of the Life and Legacy of Christ in Verse and Sculpture

Resource Publications
An Imprint of Wipf and Stock Publishers
199 W. 8th Ave., Suite 3
Eugene, OR 97401

www.wipfandstock.com

PAPERBACK ISBN: 979-8-3852-4656-4
HARDCOVER ISBN: 979-8-3852-4657-1
EBOOK ISBN: 979-8-3852-4658-8

VERSION NUMBER 07/22/25

Dedicated to all those whom I have made to think through my sermons and art forms in the hopes it has spurred your thoughts and reflections further. May these poems help others.

Contents

List of Illustrations

All sculptures by Toddy Hoare. *Where not mentioned the other sculptures are Plaster for Bronze as studio master copies for any further bronze casts within a limited edition of 9.*

Ministry.

8 Stations of the Cross. *All are 8ft X 4ft in Resin Bonded Bronze. 2005.*

Teaching.

Holy Communion.

Cover Art

The Holy Family or Flight to Egypt

This working sketch was for a bronze sculpture which I cast myself from a wax original on a course at the RA but was stolen from a gallery in Manchester, although other items were later recovered. This was also used for the relief of the same title in my Stations of the Nativity.

Fishing Boat in Christ's Time

This fishing boat is drawn on the stonework in the old quarry below the Church of the Holy Sepulchre in Jerusalem where it is believed the disciples and co. had a fish shop. It was unearthed by a friend, Archie Walls, in the early 1970s when working for the British School of Archaeology out there under Crystal Bennett.

Foreword

SOME PEOPLE STRIKE YOU immediately as rooted in the land. Jesus must have encountered many such people, and the Greek work *agrous* (Mark 5 14, 6 36, 6 56, 10 29–30) describes the country (sometimes translated farms), where the herdsmen of the pigs (Mark 5 14), or simply the country people (Mark 6 36) lived. Jesus related to them intimately. So too in England the 'country parson' is a well-known figure, with a country church, and deep knowledge of animals, and farming. When I first met Toddy in 1988, I straightaway knew he was a country parson, who eventually spent twenty-four years on the North Yorkshire Moors caring for his flock. Another of his essays, *The Wagging Tail,* had a preface by Robin Hanbury Tennison of the Countryside Alliance, speaking of the qualities of a good parson: "humility, a sense of perspective and . . . understanding human nature". Toddy stands in the long tradition of the country parson, compassionate and wise, from George Herbert, David Scott, to R.S. Thomas, all clergy of, and literally in, the field, visiting their people, farmers, labourers, the people of the moors.

How then can one express this love of Jesus, love of people and love of the countryside, animals and crops, so much written deep within the heart of the country parson? First, Toddy turned to sculpture, which he was trained in as a student, and on his days off in the parish he sculpted many biblical pieces, as well as busts of the friends he knew. I have prayed so many times in front of these sculptures as principal of a theological college, gazed on them in the fading light at evensong, seen religious leaders taken aback by the sculpture of Mary Magdalene, felt sympathy for (but also strongly dissuaded) deeply pious students who wanted to cover the breasts and genitalia because these sculptures were in a chapel. I have been moved by them with deep inward affection (*splagchna* Phil 2 1), because they show human life at its most earthy, visceral, the result of the incarnation. They have spoken to my gut of God giving himself to the people of Galilee and Jerusalem in the incarnation.

And in retirement Toddy has turned to poetry alongside the sculpture, a direct evocation of the birth of Jesus , with his words *"Woman stands easing the strain of frontal fulness, energy metabolised, programmed to nurture "*, meditating on Jesus the Good Shepherd *"His sheep know his old coat, recognise familiar noise of paper sack"*, the death of Jesus *"When a babe taking a nourished rest, now dies a lingering terrorist's death, that they in turn mete out, vile brothers,"* and the presence of Christ in Holy Communion *"The Cup of Wrath becomes the Cup of Salvation"*. Each poem has a sculpture that fits it profoundly. It has taken a lifetime of ministry, of sculpture, of preaching, to produce this small book. It is a "communion with God's creation", by one who knows God deeply and has made him known in his life. May this book speak to you in your heart, deeply, and with profound emotion.

Peter Sedgwick
Church of the Resurrection, Cardiff
Ash Wednesday 2025

Acknowledgments

I MUST THANK ALL those who from theological college onwards have given me food for thought along with many worthy preachers who have broken open the Word for me, especially those I made an effort to travel and hear. I must also add thanks for the gentle guidance into better theology I received at the feet of Anthony Hanson who was my honorary curate during his retirement and always made a point of starting chapter meetings with Bible Study which in turn set a perspective and often answers for any business that followed. I would also like to acknowledge thankfully Peter Sedgwick who guided me through theological reflection on the MA course at Hull University that Anthony Hanson had set up, A Theological Understanding of Industrial Society. Lastly I must give credit to my wife, Liz, with whom I share ministry and a love of the Bible and the Word, who keeps me on my toes.

Introduction

THE CHRIST CYCLE IS a collection of poems as food for thought, illustrated with my sculpture, that I have written in the last two decades reflecting on the Christian story both when I have had to write a sermon and have not been on duty so not needed to write a sermon. I have themed it through the liturgical year with some parallel thoughts from the Old Testament background, and finished with reflections on Holy Communion. It is there for any Christian at any stage or depth of their journey of belief and faith to find a prompt for thought or an evening prayer or to have a reminder of the current theme at whatever time it is in the liturgical year. It draws heavily on three cycles of Stations; The Stations of the Cross; The Stations of the Nativity; and what are left of the Stations of the Call of the Disciples, which after some 20 years on public display at Burton Agnes Hall in the East Riding of Yorkshire had to be scrapped. Arts Council grants had paid for two sabbatical projects while a parish priest to make the first and the third sets. It entailed biblical research of the gospels which in turn has fuelled further poetic musings on the gospels, the life of Christ, and how we might take thought for the major seasons or festivals. In part the poems are summaries of how the subject matter struck me and the poems are illustrations of the same over 40 years of ministry. Best described as a hors d'oeuvre to further study, reading and reflection. I have given all the Bible references so the real narrative can be found and digested.

Toddy Hoare
Danby Wiske, North Yorkshire, 25/2/25

Introduction. Psalm 147.

It brings joy to the heart to offer thanks
And praise to the Lord who has established
Jerusalem* and scoops up the outcast.
He heals the broken-hearted and sick. Past
Number are the stars but named as He wished
In His infinite wisdom. Heathen ranks
He brings down but makes the meek stand upright.
He waters the earth, grass and herbs flourish
So man and beast feed, even ravens do.
He secures Sion*, her children within too.
Frost, ice and snow obey His every wish:
Peace and prosperity become birthright.
What other nation enjoys such attention?
Of His laws the heathen make no mention.

*Means Place of Peace.

Nativity

The Stations of the Nativity in 8 panels.

The Annunciation. Matthew 1,vv18-25. Luke 1, vv26-38.

What if?' thought the young girl gazing
In a mirror and seeing herself change
In her mind's eye swollen with child.
How could it be without a man? Wild
Behaviour—led astray—maybe baby: range
Of options where some girls do. Amazing
Thoughts but as a social outcast life
Would not be easy unless as a wife
Security was found to nurture a son,
Assuming down paths matrimonial
That journey already had begun.
Without nuptial ceremonial,
If practiced, children appeared none the worse,
So where's God's part in scripture, chapter, verse?

The Annunciation. 1st Station. (What if? & How?) Bronze diptych relief.

With Child.

(Nativity and crucifixion. Alpha & Omega. A beginning and an end.)

Woman stands easing the strain of frontal fulness,
Energy metabolised, programmed to nurture
The child within, which soon will feed.
Mother's breasts swollen to meet need
To suckle, to contentment an overture;
Sleep comes mouth feeling full, not restless,
Leaving years of a falling sensation
From being laid down. Maternal care
Supports shy toddler unsure of play.
Were these Jerusalem women on the way
To Golgotha whom Jesus addressed aware
Of his past and present destination?
Denied such peace as on a mother's breast
Till with death he enters God promised rest.

With Child.

8

Magnificat. 2nd Station of the Nativity. Luke 1, vv46–56.

Mary to Elizabeth made haste:
It was of pregnancy their first taste.
As agents of God's will Word became life
To change the world where sinful man was rife.
'My soul magnifies the Lord, glad to find
Him my saviour, to His handmaid kind.
All will see me blessed, His name bringing changes
As human values He re-arranges.
The world topsy-turvy, human hearts revealed,
He knows in whom His promises are sealed.
The rich put in place, tumbled the grand,
Daily bread feeds the hungry on demand.
He brings mercy to all who'd embrace it,
And hope to the poor unable to face it.'

Anticipating the Cry of John the Baptist. Luke 3, vv1–23.

Repent, repent, the Kingdom's nigh
Turn back to your Lord on high.
Re-enter now the Promised Land
Receive those Blessings freely given
Salvation of souls is now at hand.
Serve God alone with conscience clear
Washing off all sin in Jordan River.
Soon will come the Spirit giver
Power from high to daunt all fear.
Come too the Kingdom of Heaven
Where God's will is done by all
Restoring the children of the fall.
Thus John the Baptist launched the way
That none from God might further stray.

Magnificat. 2nd Station of the Nativity. Luke 1, vv46–56.

The Nativity, Birth. 3rd Station.

Matt1, vv18–25. Luke 2, vv1–7.

When the waters broke no-one was there
The main room of the house was occupied. Here
We had that human space where, a bit rough,
The beasts laid or fed from a trough.
No mid-wife nor birthing stool
So I knelt and spread my thighs:
Thus Mary perched to deliver her baby;
I put pressure downwards on her shoulders
To help her push each contraction.
Being young she gave birth easily,
All happening with hardly a cry.
She held the child to her breast,
Too soon to feed until lactation,
But with joy and satisfaction,
So she wrapped him tightly
In her cloak while I strawed
A manger as a warming bed.
The beasts endorsed with their presence
Our basic nature raised by faithful sense.
Tired, she fell asleep with a smile,
Her head tilted against my side, while
I sat watching the bright moonlight outside
But an inner radiance came from the child.

The Birth 3 ex 8 Stations of the Nativity.

The Shepherds.

The Shepherds Call, 4 ex 8 Stations of the Nativity. Luke 2, vv8–20.

They sought the truth these shepherd strangers
Alert to birth and new-born life. Hearing
Cries heralding life had made a new start
Laid amongst the troughs and mangers.
Their rough accents belied a warmth of heart
To check that all was well since God-fearing
Folk wished all neighbours well however mean
Their circumstances. Their needs would be met,
The good news told, for even the heavens seemed
Alive to sing celestially what people dreamed.
Not just lambs; life itself did God beget,
A very mystery demanding, when seen,
Nurture such as shepherds knew to give
That the Word of God and truth might live.

The Shepherds Call.

The Magi.

5 ex 8 Stations of the Nativity, Matthew 2, vv1–12.

Wise men, we don't know how many
Sought a child, but not just any
Their astrology and calculations
Led to their perambulations.

Coming from out the East to see
Pointed to a scion of Jesse
They followed bright stars' alignment
To Mary in her confinement.

Stars as arranged their indication,
Herod's team gave validation.
Scriptures searched soon revealed
Where the promise might be sealed.

The old fox's cunning they distrusted
Since for rivals' death he lusted;
Unaware of their complicity
They fuelled tyrant insecurity.

In their wake their straight sagacity
Fired his rage so implicitly
He killed in retaliation
Babies without hesitation.

Bethlehem their destination
Imagine their elation
Finding in this situation
The child of reconciliation.

They approached surroundings shambolic
Offering gifts greatly symbolic
Gold for kingship would render
Solvency where means were slender.

Frankincense with pleasing odour
Symbolised priestly prayers of candour;
Myrrh a disinfectant of old
Martyrdom to follow foretold.

So satisfied by what they found
Knowing their wisdom was that sound
The Magi went upon their way,
Joseph and Mary showed no dismay.

In turn the Holy Family left,
Herod left some mothers bereft
Of babes, refugees Egypt bound
Keeping the Christ child safe and sound.

The Visit of the Magi. 5 ex 8 Stations of the Nativity.

Candlemas. Luke 2. vv22-28.

Presentation Of The Christ Child In The Temple. 6 ex 8 Stations
of the Nativity.

The old seer, Simeon, took the child yielded
By his mother come to give thanks flanked
By her caring husband—not all sharing
Duties required from parents God fearing.
With birth the mother's pregnancy ceased
So this child represented from service released.
Death to old ways, fresh starts, so God be thanked
Raising aloft like an offering fielded
This babe that answered a life-time's prayer,
Shining as light in the world, revelation
That God at last ushered in salvation
For all to share his glory. No sooth-sayer
Could predict as much which Anna echoed
That this child God's redemption showed.

Presentation of Christ in the Temple. Bronze Triptych.

Motherhood.

Nursing Mother.

Nursing Mother.

With their breasts heavy with nourishment
Mothers are pictures of contentment
Feeding their infants crooked in their arms.
Discomfort of swollen bellies, back ache,
Labour pains hopefully forgotten;
Spent effort for those begotten.
Images of those after whom they take
Wait before others see those charms
Appear. Meanwhile maternal days
Are marked by a new fulfilment
While her body, with a new dependent,
Continues in another phase
To meet demands of bonding,
Changing, feeding, responding.

Flight to Egypt.

7 ex 8 panels of The Stations of the Nativity. Matthew 2, vv13–18.

Instinct told Joseph something was amiss.
He must hasten mother and new-born child
To safety, since something displayed by word
In the Magi's manner of what they heard
In Jerusalem left him chilled,
For Herod would not bend to greet and kiss
A boy hailed as king but a sword would bring
To remove a rival. He saddled his ass.
Egypt beckoned, a safe destination,
Where with skills it was his intention
To be the carpenter to whom this lass
Was betrothed with a view to supporting
Instant family, bringing security.
Now, more than saving face, he was surety.

The Flight to Egypt. (Triptych.)

24

Boy Jesus in the Temple.

8 ex 8 Stations of the Nativity. Luke 2, vv41–52.

Where can he be? fretted the anxious Mum;
Journeying home with friends he'd not been seen.
What fate awaited a boy not street wise
If he'd stayed in Jerusalem with no ties
To wider family? Looking where they'd been,
Back-tracking to the Temple they were struck dumb
To find crowds listening with intent
To a boy quizzing the priests with aplomb.
He seemed to step out from scripture so sure
Answering his own points with sense so pure,
Covering psalm-like life from birth to tomb
Obedient to God as scripture meant.
His Father's business was his excuse
Not roaming Jerusalem on the loose.

Boy Jesus in the Temple.

Baptism.

While Matthew and Luke start with Jesus' physical birth and include his Baptism Mark and John start their gospels with Christ's spiritual birth so to speak at his baptism, the mechanics of which, even today, I would compare with Jacob's experience of wrestling with God, Genesis 32, vv22–32.

Jacob Wrestling.

Jacob wrestled with his conscience and the Word of God;
Forced to face himself he found himself lacking.
He needed to reform, favourite of mother,
A rotten cheat who usurped his brother
Whom he feared to encounter next day
Having sent family and flocks safely away:
Esau might even send him packing
Unlikely to return a brotherly nod.
He crossed the Jabbok, running water, inference
Of the waters of Baptism. Called by a new name,
Israel, he walked with limping difference,
Relationships with Self, God and Brother not the same.
Jacob is born again spiritually complete
Renewed inner confidence whoever he might meet.

Jacob Wrestling. Bronze.

Finding Christ

Where the Closed Old Church Stood.

Where the old medieval church stood
Remains a thin place with graves old and new
And a stand of yews replicates the site
As if the church was ever green, its height
Reflected by trees of a different hue,
And width by the density of this wood.
No entrance nor exit marks this place
Keeping secret its sacred space
Nor indicating nave or chancel, vestry,
Tower if one stood, or sanctuary.
No mark remains of the actual spot
Nor specific features enclose the plot
Where worship and prayers ascended.
Only echos that what was once hasn't ended.

The Call of the Disciples

Philip & Nathanael.

Under the Fig Tree. John 1, vv43–51. (Compare Psalm 32.)

Philip brought his friend Nathanael bread
Finding him neath fig trees spread.
He had no care for what Philip said
Men from Galilee were as good as dead.
Yet this new found bloke seemed divine
Discerning Nathanael's confession
And knowing his prayers as if present:
An Israelite without guile, he liked his style.
He would tarry and listen awhile.
His harvest ladder proved a prop, leant
Against the trees, for further revelation.
He felt forgiven, perking up, life was fine.
Of impending Cana nuptials no mention
But his was psalmist's talk not mere invention.

Philip finds Nathanael.

The Zealots.

Simon the Canaanite & Judas Iscariot.

(The Sicarii or Dagger men, or Zealots since they would fight the Romans.)

Matthew 10, v4; 26, vv21–25. Mark 14, vv18–21. Luke 22, vv21–23. John 13, vv21–30.

(NB. In John Judas is dismissed before the Last Supper Discourses and Prayers, 14–17.)

The Zealots were strange recruits
Amongst the summoned twelve
Unlikely to find that such Good News suits
Their different message from dig and delve
With no paradise gained instead.
Ambushes, assassinations, thefts were their game
And it seemed good sense to use Jesus' name.
Rebellion was a different cause with Romans dead.
Could they force his hand, make him king?
Could Simon and Judas make him bring
To fruition the kingdom he proclaimed?
Surely from what he says he must be named?
Was he naive, might play into their hand
As they sought to force their Promised Land?

The Zealots.

Sons of Zebedee.

James and John. Matthew 4, vv18–25.
(Sons of Thunder, Boanerges, Mark 3, v17; 9, vv38–41;Luke 9, vv51–56. Matthew 20, vv20–28; Mark 10, vv35–45.)

Expecting a catch Zebedee put to sea.
Sons James and John strained hard
To launch the boat from the shore,
Leaving Dad with the hired hands.
They were set to follow this new Rabbi
Who offered new hopes, new life and more
Than family fishing could ever bring.
Certainly they would be aboard his boat
When Israel was restored; now there's a thing!
Power would keep this new kingdom afloat;
These Sons of Thunder might gain position
Sweeping aside all opposition.
They found instead of mending every net
They amended their ways—a far safer bet!

James & John launch Zebedee.

42

Mary Magdalen, the First Apostle.

Mary Magdalen. (The Person.)

Mary Magdalen.

Many Marys made their mark
Not least the Magdalen, maid
Maybe mother, exposed and stark,
Sicut Lilium, recognition made
The garden of sorrows a delight,
Though Mark records they ran in fright,
To find her Lord restored for evermore.
Commissioned apostle news to tell
She has witnessed that all is well,
No need to go to Galilee shore.
Of her past there's so little we know
Save that she was a lady of means
Following the Lord where he might go
Supplying more than empty dreams.
Seven devils—who knows what kind?
Mary Magdalen restored in mind.

Mary Magdalen. Not a prostitute, though sometimes confused with Mary of the immoral woman who anointed Jesus' feet. Compare Luke 8, vv1–3 with Matthew 26, vv6–13 and Mark 14, vv3–9 (feet anointed by Mary of Bethany), Luke 7, vv36–50 and John 12, vv1–8.

The first to see the risen Lord Jesus, John 20, vv1–18, and be sent to tell the others (the criteria to be an apostle!)

Ministry

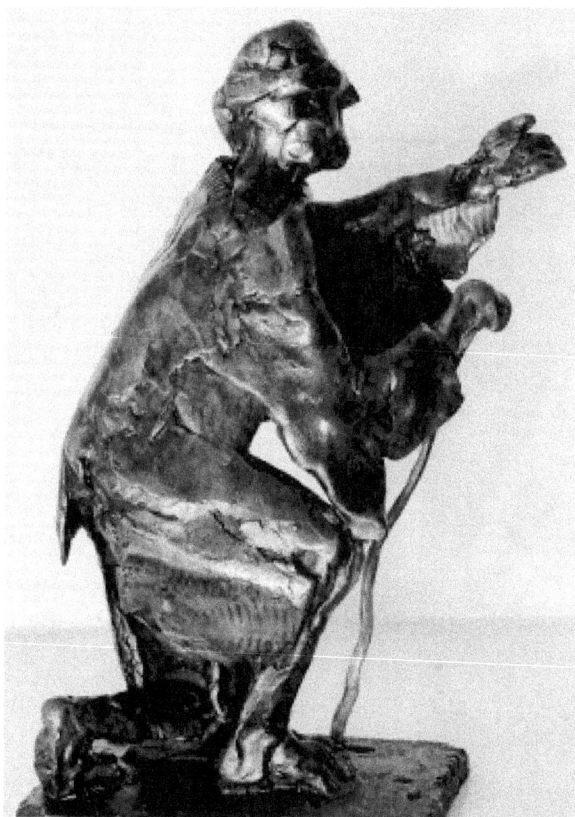

Blind Bart. Bronze.

Blind Bart, Healing.

Seeing and Seeing. Mark 10, vv46–52.

When Blind Bartimaeus called out
All eyes turned on him. Was his chance denied?
'Don't trouble him', 'Hold your tongue,' they cried.
Remarks that made him louder shout.
He sensed his call for help was heard.
After being led over as requested
And asked what it was he wanted
To regain sight seemed not absurd.
He didn't want his eyes to be tested
And his request was soon granted;
No spit; no parental blame; no game;
No men seen walking like trees; no shame.
With this symbolic act Jesus let men see
That his ministry was reality.

The Good Shepherd. John 10, vv1–18.

His sheep know his old coat, recognise
Familiar noise of paper sack
Rattling contents of nuts of some kind.
Calls heard none inclined to lag behind
Following their shepherd pack on back,
Just mouthfuls each judging by its size.
Animal husbandry at best
Often takes the simplest form
Nurturing beasts without fear,
Ensuring food is always near,
Shelter from any passing storm,
Safety when laid down to digest.
By such means the priest takes stock
Entrusted by God to care for his flock.

The Good Shepherd. Bronze.

The Transfiguration.

Matthew 17, vv1–13. Mark 9, vv2–13. Luke 9, vv28–36.

Raised above daily business below
Mountain top panoramas show
A world to command as Satan
Had suggested in the wilderness.
Now Jesus with his chosen three
Seeks a seal on his ministry
With them present there to witness
What Moses and Elijah began.
Shining whiter than the best on earth
Three stood transfigured to discuss
A particular exodus
Adding to the Word greater worth
Prefiguring glory when heaven
Descended on mankind with new leaven.

The Transfiguration.

Since Jesus encountered Moses and Elijah during the Transfiguration to discuss his exodus spare a thought for both.

Moses at the burning bush encounters God.

Exodus 3.

Moses shoeless stood on holy ground,
The burning bush unconsumed found:
Sign that God would deliver from bondage
A populous people, slavery their wage.
Though Moses daren't look directly for shame
When God spoke to reveal his name,
Future and present, a basic verb, will and am.
This bush symbolises the Virgin born lamb,
Whose unquenchable flame reaches into our spiritual life.
Seneh, bramble, monastery bound round Sinai cliff
Is called Rebus Sanctus, not the gas plant Diptam,
Dictamnus Albus, with too short lived flame,
This glory, uncreated energies of God, shows His face,
Logos, His Word, and saving grace for a chosen race.

Water from rock.

Exodus 17, vv1–7.

Layers of settling sediment with different tone
Over many millennia smothered old rock,
By sheer weight compressed to porous sandstone.
Minerals dissolve, accumulate, blocking water in faults
Until the crusted deposits on strata edges were struck
By Moses' staff; water flowed on dislodging the salts.
In wadis hungry Israelite refugees pluck
The white crystallised flowers from the Rumph plant
Now enjoyed by camels but once as manna food stock
Nourishing a nation that at God would rant.
While atop Sinai strange natural action
Produces letter-like patterns, the citation
Of law giving tablets for social application.
This practical explanation gave spiritual direction.

Elijah encountered the still small voice (utter silence) of God at Horeb (desolation) 1 Kings 19, vv9–18.

Is God futuristic? In the end—God?
Emptied to nothing do we encounter nothing?
Jesus emptied himself for us: with us does God rest?
Elijah was empty and found utter silence.
God is in the Nothing from which He created,
A Primum Mobile with a spirit of movement
Bringing all together in a Word on the nod.
The world became alive and mankind initiated
If prepared to have life abundantly in that sense
The Son intended, source of discernment
To seek the truth, live with joy, avoiding test
And time of trial, rooting our ethics ever since
In Christian values lived out and taught
Yet on the Cross finally bought.

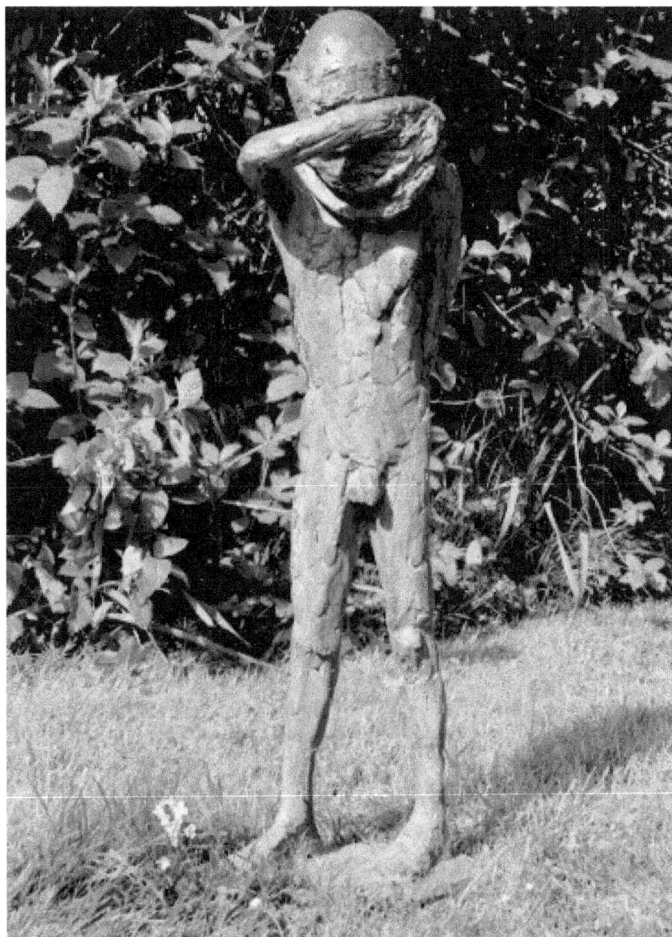

Elijah encounters the still small voice.

The 8 Stations of the Cross.

1st Station. Jesus is Condemned.

Matthew 27, vv11–26. Mark 15, vv2–15. Luke 23, vv3–25. John 18, vv29–40.

Dragged from prayer on a trumped up charge
All the priests condemn Jesus for his claim
Then put him before Pilate who finds no blame.
His wife sends her maid with warning
Before truth to Pilate started dawning.
Jesus points out authority comes from above
Not music to the ears of priests lacking love
Who out of enmity want him killed
Heedless of those he cured and storms he stilled.
Thus a terrorist is set at large
After betrayal in Gethsemane willingly lured.
Fundamentalism will reduce all to dust.
Hands washed to prove innocence and disgust
Letting perverted justice prove priests' verdict unjust.

Jesus is condemned,

2. Jesus is Led Away.

Matthew 27, vv32–44. Mark 15, vv21–32. Luke 23, vv32–43. John 19, vv17–24.

Jesus condemned is led away
Weakened by mocking, appearance shocking.
Soldiers compel a passer-by to carry
His cross to Golgotha where nailed
He'll hang until dead, cruelly impaled.
Simon of Cyrene rises to the task
Not the sort of occurrence soldiers ask
Others politely to do. Coercion is their way
With kicks and curses; it's their lot today.
The lowest denominator leads to bestial
Behaviour where life is forfeit, trumping fair trial
When the Word uttered no word.
To those who followed it seemed absurd
No defence made, no support heard.

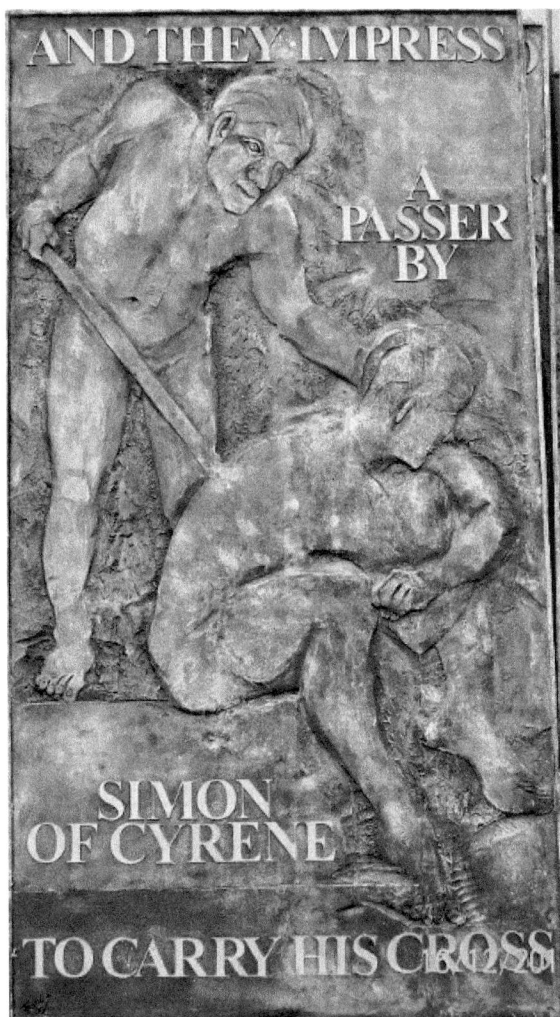

AND THEY IMPRESS A PASSER BY SIMON OF CYRENE TO CARRY HIS CROSS

Jesus is led away.

3, The Women of Jerusalem.

Luke 23, vv26–31.
(Depicted as a mother & toddler group to also link nativity to resurrection.)

Without the city wall mothers gather watching,
Considered unclean this group their toddlers raise:
The next generation while the world spins on.
Addressed by Jesus "Daughters of Jerusalem"
He bids them weep for themselves, not him,
Their children, and dark days ahead.
Injustice is beyond their power to relieve
Yet gives birth to a faith where they believe
That salvation is for the soul not ritual,
Temple and rigid observance of the virtual
Where God is lost in petty laws and rules.
Tithe the heart to pay your dues, forgive
Those trespassing your personal space
Making room for the workings of God's grace.

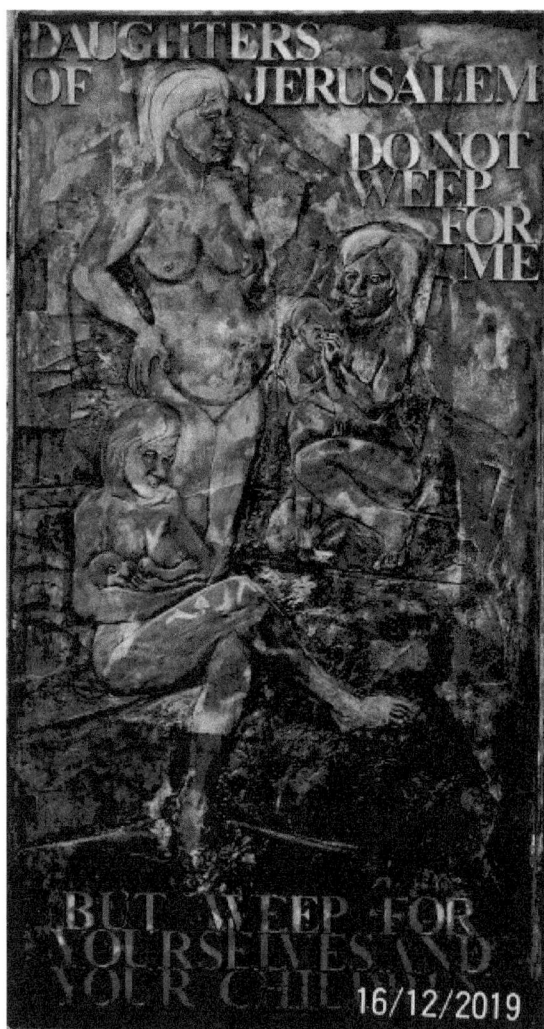

The Women of Jerusalem.

4. Jesus is Crucified.

Matthew 27, vv32–44. Mark 15, vv21–32. Luke 23, vv32–43.
John19, vv17–24.

Ignorant of the implication of their actions
Roman soldiers nail Jesus to the cross.
Triumphant Pharisees gloat and mock
Exonerated by Pilate who found no crime,
Washing his hands of responsibility.
A Jewish problem for Jews to sort
Victim of abuse and public sport.
Jesus' forgiveness highlights their ignorance
Of what scriptures outlined, prophets foretold.
God's purpose works despite men's machinations.
Genesis tree through his death is life for all
Enabling discernment between good and evil, not fall.
The cruelty of man is strange contrast
To the love of God that everything will outlast.

They crucify Jesus.

5. Controversy: 5th Station of the Cross.

John 19, vv17–22. Luke 23, vv39–43.
*(Pilate and the Chief Priests argue over the words of the inscription,
and the thieves argue about guilt, punishment and salvation—where
both literal and spiritual are compared.)*

To your mortal end you still caused strife.
Confessing just desserts the guilty thief
Found a saviour alongside promising eternal relief.
T' other thief challenged Christ demanding life
While on the ground chief priests disputed
Over Pilate's triple notice stating
This innocent man in the middle was reputed
The King of the Jews, so past debating.
Barabbas the terrorist was released
The crowd conned by confusion of his name—
As Son of the Father it seemed the same—
Claiming familiarity with God never ceased.
The cross raised endless more controversy
'Mongst disbelievers showing no mercy.

Controversy.

6. They Cast Lots for his Clothes.

Matthew 27, vv35–36. Psalm 22, v18. John 19, vv23–24; 28–30.
Luke 23, v47.*

'Truly this was the Son of God' first
The Centurion, convinced witness, claimed.
Had God deserted the Divine at the last?
Was all in vain? The human exclaimed "I thirst."
'My God, why hast thou forsaken me?' Shamed,
Suggestive of passing doubt in divine purpose?
While soldiers fulfilled scripture of old,
Lots for the victim's clothes are cast,
Step by step we see his life unfold.
The Psalms come to gruesome life stage
By stage on the stage of Golgotha's scull.
Man's angst is at a scapegoat aimed.
The seamless garment's winner we'll never know
Though other winners the cross does show.

* *This is an autobiographical touch in the figure in the panel and myself having been a soldier.*

They cast lots for his clothes.

7. Women at the Foot of the Cross.*

Matthew 27, vv55–56. Mark 15, vv40–41. Luke 23, v49. John 19, vv25–27.

Like the three graces with their chaperone
Stand silent the Three Marys and Salome,
Supportive women and sorrowing Mother
Of whom he is mindful to hand to another.
Unable to intervene, just watch and pray
While Jesus' life, agony riven, ebbs away;
A lonely vigil these four must keep.
This medium of the Saviour's birth
Replaced the figure of Mother Earth.
Perhaps the Magdalen with her ability
Epitomises the Word's fertility
And revelations of truths so deep.
Literally on the Word they wait
While Jesus is obedient to his fate.

*This is a parody on the 3 graces, Mary Magdalen centre and Mary the Mother of Jesus behind as the chaperone and a Mother Earth figure since Greek Mythology always depicted her clothed as opposed to the nakedness of those representing fertility.

The women at the foot of the cross.

8. Jesus Risen.

Matthew 28, vv1–10. Mark 16, vv1–8. Luke 24, vv1–11. John 20, vv1–10.

Thomas overcame his doubts, pragmatic to the last.
While needing proof he remained aloof
Being privileged to witness Jesus in the flesh.
Others at Emmaus recognised,
Bemused by the truths of scripture,
The familiar breaking of bread,
When the light dawned and all fell into place.
A fleeting encounter proved death's grip
Couldn't hold the real risen presence.
Revelation came in an upper room
Before giving trusted friends the slip.
The shared reality of Good News
Gave them hope and reasons for belief.
That all wasn't in vain dispelled their grief.

Jesus risen surprises one and all, both the disciples in the upper room, and those on the road to Emmaus.

Stabat Mater.

Only in John 19, vv25–27,

There stands his mother, hesitant, short of breath,
Supported afar off in her anguish by others
As her son, who once snoozed upon her breast
When a babe taking a nourished rest,
Now dies a lingering terrorist's death,
That they in turn mete out, vile brothers,
To those of a different persuasion.
His crucified body on his deposition
Will have a final maternal embrace
With kisses on his disfigured face;
Actions as sharp as piercing sword.
Your grief is ours for one adored.
Where in such sorrow can grace reside
Escaping death's dominion that love abide?

Stabat Mater.

Good Friday, 7//4/23. & last words summarized.
Psalm22,v1. John 19, v30.

Stirred by those who rejected you, of a different stance,
Meant those who on Palm Sunday regaled you
Became the ones who on the cross nailed you.
Yet you forgave their ignorance.
You accepted one thief to Paradise restored
As to a son you presented the Mother you adored.
Of course you must have felt forsaken:
Where is God when your life is taken?
Indeed you thirst, you, the living water,
Thirst for others to know truth through your pain.
Your work is finished on earth. To live again
In your failure is our success without falter.
In your destruction we new creation take.
You commit to the Father who gives to make.

Grief.

Is the agony of grief the greater
Because I am spared or left?
Is the pain sword thrust in Mary's heart,
Despite warning, that she and son must part?
Can greater sorrow than the cross leave one so bereft?
Yet grief, like Gethsemane, bleeds sooner or later.
Hours of vigil cause mounting tension,
Prompt denial, disbelief, generate reaction
Weighing down the weary shattered soul.
While reluctant truth accepts reality. A hole
Against increasing pain's accumulation
Opens within so life seems spent in suspension.
When heart and mind differently act
Memory accommodates the fact.

His Grief on Thursday. Her Grief on Friday. Bronze.

At the Empty Tomb. (The Setting.)

Mary Magdalen.
Matthew 28,vv1–10. Mark16, vv1–8. Luke 24, vv1–11. John 20, vv1–18.

Silence is broken, empty space redeemed.
No good looking in an empty tomb
But move on to where life teamed.
Away with long faces and gloom.
Mark recounts " Go tell the disciples" (who fail to see)
"I am going before you to Galilee."
The women fled petrified after one look.
Luke poses differently in his book
"Why seek ye the living amongst the dead?"
They told the disciples so Peter ran ahead.
Matthew tells us the Marys find
The tomb is empty and are assigned
To tell the disciples Galilee is where
They will encounter their Master dear.
John fills out the picture even more:
Mary Magdalen no gardener saw
But surprised by Jesus to her relief,
Is warned ere ascension not to cling.
What change in the Son had God begun?
Her report causes Peter and John to run
And see for themselves this challenging thing.
Bold Peter enters first. John finds belief.

The Ascension.

Luke 24, vv50–53. Acts 1, vv9–11.
(Mark 16, vv19–20 Maybe a later addition if Mark finished at v8)

At the Transfiguration* all synoptics agree
That Moses, Elijah and Jesus discussed as three
His exodus on conclusion of earthly ministry.
Crucifixion, an appalling prospect, would free
The path from special birth to resurrection.
Such prospectus needed a termination
After the legacy of communion to combine
The sacred and the mortal through bread and wine,
Though John's quenching vinegar was ironic
Since dead wine is hardly a pick-me-up tonic.
To raise the spirits the Spirit must rise,
Ascension would be quite a surprise
But not leave a relic for wars or worship.
Memorial celebrations are no hardship.

* Might the raising of Lazarus in John match it as out of this world?

Christ's Legacy

Holy Communion. Psalms 16; 75, vv9–10; Isaiah 51, vv17–23; Matt 26, v39.

Rev 14, v10; Matt 26, vv26–29/Mark 14, vv22–25/ Luke 22, vv19–24. (John 13,vv21–30. 15.)

1 Cor. 11, v25.

The Blessing: Truth and Beauty.

If true beauty eternal be
What of lovely things I see?
While much in the beholder's eye
Is classed beautiful it won't last
Or ephemeral will be past
As a mood; those we love will die.
But he who died has true beauty
Though there is no record of his looks;
Images can only prompt the mind
To discern his teaching and find
Through a wealth of thoughts and books
That he is the very Word of God.
Invisible such beauty stays present
In response to Christ whom God's love sent.

In the light of Resurrection.

Luke 24, vv1–7.

Resurrection.

Two men in bright white said "He has risen,
He is not here." They bade those women sad
Return to tell the disciples they would see,
Despite hesitating, Jesus in Galilee.
Many fans would think them quite mad:
The dead don't return as if arisen.
Why do you seek the living among the dead?
It all seems strange, hard to believe;
The impossible is overcome with faith,
Mystery remains not worship of a wraith.
Holy Spirit will the despondent relieve
Don't you remember what he said?
He's risen indeed is our Easter cry
How we live must be our reply.

Pentecost.

Acts 2, vv 1–13 (—v47 for the whole experience,)

What were those tongues of flame like fire
That descended from way above?
Perhaps a flickering Holy Dove
Changing overhead auras of the crowd
Enabling talk in divers languages out loud;
Holy Spirit will others inspire.
This heavenly fiery sign of power
Energizes open minds to fresh
Wisdom giving all a context
Where Jesus lives in each. There follows next
Peace that passes all understanding. Flesh
Contains strength like the psalmist's tower.
Communication of Good News knows
No bounds as Holy Spirit's grace flows.

Advent. (2024)

Isaiah 7, vv10–17. Matthew 1, 18–25. Luke 1, vv26–38.

Advent I.

Do we heed the prophet's cry
That the Lord our God is nigh?
Are we ready to repent
For our world to make lament?
Do we wait with baited breath
That there's more to life than death?
Is our response joy to the world
That peace and love are unfurled?
John's message hope will bring,
While Mary's Son gives teaching
Of a way to be, God's image
As the Word revealed page by page.
Waiting is preparation
To receive our salvation.

Advent II.

The Christmas earworm strikes again.
Annual pre-amble to Christ's reign
As carols jump the Advent gun.
Once more the waiting has begun.
Stop, listen, let the music speak:
Prayerful choirs of Oxford seek
T' summon us advent-wards in psalms.
'Nd Cambridge carols raise open arms.
Joy in the son, Mary's delight,
Let's be worthy, children of light
Find comfort in the Holy Word,
Sharing with others what she heard.
In the prophets the Word found voice
But now made flesh we must rejoice.

Teaching.

John 8 vv 1—12. Woman Taken in Adultery.

Caught in the very act they claimed.
Voyeurs, they must have lain in wait.
Why stone her without including him?
She despatched he not even named.
Was this justice or a convenient bait
To catch out a Rabbi with their whim?
"It is written" he wrote in the dust.
What?! He countered their blood-lust.
"Let him without sin cast the first stone."
One by one they melt away frightened
Weary of blood-guilt. Their noose tightened
Round their own necks. So left alone
Jesus charged her to sin no more,
Find inner peace, saved by the Law.

The woman taken in adultery. *(The Hebrew written in the dust translates 'It is written.')*

Better Values.

My love for Jesus remains as man to man
AGAPE rather than EROS
But to the Holy Spirit it's answering
To her call as man to woman.
As Trinity cannot be separated
Into parts dividing the unity
So love needs containing within passion
A hint of the realities behind Baptism.
Not running carnally amok
Bridging what Greek describes
As individual characteristics
Components of the whole:
Our one word LOVE too easily
Erodes beyond the meaning meant.
In translation much more is lent.

Lazarus, the Disciple whom Jesus Loved.

John 11 v3,36; 13 v23; 19 v26; 20 v2; 21, v7,20.

They told Jesus 'He whom you love is ill,'
But he delayed three days and found him dead.
Deeply moved 'See how he loved him,' they said.
Commanded 'Lazarus come forth' the tomb he left.
Reclining close at dinner he asked who will
Betray Jesus who passed the sop. Bereft
At the foot of the cross bidden alone
To care for Jesus' mother as his own.
Faster than Peter he saw and believed;
Seeing folded grave clothes all doubts relieved.
He recognised Jesus on the shore
When their fishing nets could hold no more.
Curious, once dead would he die again?
Answer: 'Until I come he's to remain.'

John 1, v5. The light shines in the darkness, and the darkness comprehended it not.

The Darkness comprehendeth not the Light.
Light understands dark whereby we see and know
Recognising truth and naming creation
As Adam at the beginning station
When God formed other life and creatures low
Having separated day from night.
This light was embraced by the Word as life
Revealing truth, grace, and God's love for all.
The Word became flesh through Incarnation
Matched at mortal end by resurrection.
Those disciples who answered Jesus' call
Preached his Word as peace amongst worldly strife
That those accepting him him become, then led,
Spared all judgement, at communion fed.

A Word in Time .

The Word was reason to distinguish
Good from evil, and had hung on the tree
To enlighten those who ate, let them see
With opened eyes to choose and discern God's wish
For honest appreciation, company
Best understood as adoration.
The Word as flesh is impeccable, unblemished,
Personable, persuasive, undiminished,
Enabling trust to sift advantageous from harm
Using our freewill Godwards, without alarm,
Weighing the odds in considered moderation
As conscience, soul, and rationality
Dictate within individual experience:
Sure fruit expressing truth and sense.

Finding the Glory.

A Listening Church.

The Church is called to be different
Yet take people as she finds,
Prepared to go against the flow
To weigh with God others' problems
By listening, offering prayer, spent
To soothe and focus troubled minds,
Echoing the psalmist without show
Surrounded with doubt as life hems
In the individual pent
As relentless anxiety grinds.
Where else then can anyone go
But find peace in Wisdom's gems
Stirring the still small voice, silent
Till glory replaces lament?

Religio: Tethered or Bound?

(Matt. 11, vv28–30.)

What freedoms do we know through faith?
Is it an anchor to hold avast
Like boats secured against the tide
Or a tether as a horse after a ride
Is secured to feed rather than cast
Free to forage in a field. What saith
Our Lord to guide us in our lives
Rather than bind as Pharisees
Tied up the people of their day?
Secure belief is the only way
That an ordinary life, without fees
Levied on the soul for control, strives
For peace in a world self absorbed
Or unlit adrift aimless and bored.

Compassion.

Mark 5, vv21–43.

When hemmed in by crowds to be healed
Or on behalf of family who appealed
For their needs Jesus would stop, turn and yield:
By that experience their faith was sealed.
Truth was uncovered by compassion,
Of love the deepest expression.
Despite reluctance when called elsewhere
This emotion makes us stop and share.
Such is the depth of love's dimension,
Impossible to hold others in suspension
When their need cries out that we offer care
And in our hands their burden bear.
Through love of neighbour others come first
We become God's agent to slake their thirst.

False hopes v Reality.

2 Thessalonians 2, vv1–12.

Jesus ain't comin' anytime soon
Anymore than the cow jumped the moon.
Basically the reason's sad
Man is, I'm afraid, just too bad.
False prophets may predict,
Signs and outages inflict
A false sense of parousia.
We can brush up our alleluia
But until we all sing in chorus
We will remain as them and us
Without sharing a common belief
Certain Christ will bring relief.
We need a world to be as one
In peace to complete what was begun.

Transformative.

Romans 2, vv1–2 *(but vv3–21 fill out the picture more.)*

When experiencing the state of Transition
Become aware of a shift in position:
Think on passing through an opened door
You'll find life quite different from before.
Outlook and understanding change
Your focus takes on a wider range.
While a new room at first is strange
It's a certain space contained in size
Offering a new dimension wherein lies
Greater scope for life, peace not war.
Other avenues for progress light ensure,
Dialogue is possible, trust will endure.
Step forwards to reconciliation, merit;
Don't stifle that morphing transformative spirit.

Draw up a Chair

Mark 2, vv15–17. Luke 15, vv1–2; 19, vv1–10; 24, vv13–35.

I.

Who are the guests? Who's at His table?
Tax collectors and sinners
And no doubt many disable. . .d,
With others not deemed winners.
An eclectic mix across life
Of those we cross streets to avoid
Including some who stir up strife
Or might be better employed.
What an unexpected bunch to find
Yet all most welcome to sit there
Invited by our Host to be one mind
Since He of any likes to dare
Us to think things out, discover
Our response to this world's lover.

II.

It may be fine to wine and dine,
Enjoy good company and drink,
At some symposium recline
And share what others think.
What of a Host who breaks the bounds
Has open house for riff-raff 'nd knobs,
Invites whom society hounds,
And looks for what's better in yobs.
We'd be guilty to look askance
And be too choosy where to sit.
Don't overlook, a second glance
Reveals why these invitees sit:
Our Host has in mind a bigger picture
Salvation benefits quite a mixture.

A missing link.

Society needs a foundation
Of faith to live in harmony,
A fount of inspiration
Written on the heart like honey
Sweetens our everyday bread
To devour Christian values,
Because written on the heart instead
The adage governing 'you lose
I win' gains the true direction
Of worthy response to others
Underling that every action
Treats them as sisters 'nd brothers.
Listening and observation
Help spiritual formation.

Enabled to See.

Reflection and Familiarization of Isaiah 61,vv1–11.

After thought a passage for illumination
Looking to the future with anticipation
That God for Israel intends restoration
If she as a nation goes for transformation
After a period that earned her devastation.
To understand the prophecy's inspiration
God, after wilderness years, makes declaration,
Indeed He extends an invitation,
That Jesus with His divine imagination
Will live and teach a way out of desperation
And how we can become a new plantation
With a priestly role for every generation
Following repentance as a restored nation
In the light of receiving promised salvation.

The Colt, the Foal of an Ass, Important on Palm Sunday.

The excitement the occasion brought
Must have banished all thought
That I was carrying a heavy load.
Never ridden, not dismayed, no need of goad
I was chosen rather than my mother
Who had borne me, greatly burdening,
Internalised till I became other.
Previously, only a life of ease,
I had never carried anything
But today I was called to please.
Led across the valley citywards to psalms,
The going was soft, all coats and palms.
People loudly expressed their hopes realised
By the man I carried so highly prized.
Matt. 21, vv1–11; Mark 11, vv1–11; Luke 19, vv29–44; John 12, vv12–19.

A Prayer for Purpose in Life.

Based on Psalms 8, 144, 80, 122.

What is life without purpose? Others.
What is purpose in life? Serve brothers.
What is Man that thou art mindful of him?
Let thy hand be upon the Son of Man
To show us the way that we may live
And not go back from the God we know,
Whose countenance makes us whole.
Jerusalem a symbol of unity and peace
Whose prosperity we promote
Since she is the source where Word became flesh.
You remembered him and looked after him
At whose hand there was understanding
With healing for all of mankind
Who keep Jerusalem in mind.

Musing on Death.

What is death for mortals but a conveyance?
Take a new dimension, called fourth maybe,
Where we become messengers, God see,
Carrying our love in an instance.
"To see him as he is, for we (alive)
Like him shall be" to quote 1 John 3.
With instant thought sixteen we can be
Or sixty one. Might we see George Five
Face to face whose head old pennies graced?
I don't see death as darkness deep
But perpetual light, not sleep
Everlasting but a system interlaced,
Parallel without matter, increased thought
Added to the first Word that all things wrought.

What form shall I be when I depart this life?

(Based on 1 John 3, v2.)

What form shall I be when I depart this life?
I shall see him as he is, but what am I
On that last day? I shall be like him so I
See him, but not in this mortal flesh's strife
That rots away after burial. To match
Him I must what the incarnate Word became
Far removed from me, not at all the same,
As it was with resurrection to pass
Through doors or disappear,
(All flesh as for the oven is grass,)
To eat and be with those held dear
Not one for Mary Magdalen to catch.
I must be content the mystery will unfold:
Me but not me, a new substance young and old.

The True Vineyard. *(John 15.)*

True vineyards harbour the community of vines
That the Father dresses through the Word made flesh,
Discarding the fruitless and pruning the rest
That whatever is yielded is only the best.
The true vineyard's abode keeps his vines fresh
Nurtured by the Word and his wonderful signs.
This is the vintage that filled ritual jars
Their abundance bringing joy, foretelling
Harmony in the marriage of Christ and believers,
The outflowing of heavenly grace like rivers,
Forgiving our sins which blemish and life mars.
Such solid stock is rooted in truth quelling
Within that rule of self to grow as it pleases
Which used to accuse destroys like fungal diseases.

Holy Communion. The Cup of Wrath becomes the Cup of Salvation.

Psalm 75, v9. (These 5 poems reflect on this theme highlighting truth.)

God's cup of wrath had an accumulation
A reflection of His pent up frustration
With creation deserving its presentation
To drain it without interception
As their judgement and damnation.
What Son of Adam or Daughter of Eve
Could by drinking salvation achieve
Causing the cup's curse's cancellation?
The Son of Man accepted the dedication
Giving thanks with the cup's consecration
To offer all accepting eternal preservation.
Yet in Gethsemane a moment of hesitation:
'Let this cup pass, nay thy will be done'.
Thus light shone, the Kingdom was won.

Bronze Chalice.

Prophecy.

Jeremiah speaks as God told him.

'Your welfare will be what you seek, spared violation,
In foreign lands.' Like a potter discards
Malformed work so I consign you to learn
A hard lesson before regaining what you yearn.
The purchased flask is shattered into shards
To mirror in Babylon your desolation.
'I promise a good shepherd to tend my flock.
You'll return like a basket of choice figs proffered
After you drink up the cup of my wrath.
Accept my yoke lest one like iron from the north,
More harsh, will replace your rebellion. I offered
Salvation if you became purified stock.
I cut a new covenant of restoration,
Of temple worship and a mighty nation.'

Psalm 16.

I'm in Your hands, God, for You hold my trust.
My soul confesses You are my God,
Nothing else I have is of any value.
My example is that the saints have the clue
Whereas those who give false gods the nod
Can expect problems. My choice is a must
Refusing their every oblation,
Of their names I will make no mention,
For the Lord is passed on to me, the cup*
Of salvation is the true inheritance
I drink. I'm thankful the Lord holds me up,
In Him I'm certain I find life's true balance
For You spare me hell. From corruption
Your Chosen's spared, joy without interruption.

*See also Psalm 75 where the cup of judgement is offered, also Isaiah, Jeremiah, Ezekiel, Habakkuk.

Psalm 75. The cup of judgement.*

We thank You, God; Your works declare You're close.
When in charge I shall judge rightly; people shift,
They're weak so I hold them up. I tell fools
To keep Your covenant, observe the rules;
Beware of pride, shun haughtiness. No lift
In life is to be found for the morose.
God is judge as He says and He decides
Who to promote or put down. Their merits
Are weighed. He holds a cup full of red wine
From which He pours: for the elect it's fine,
The ungodly get the dregs. Their spirits
Fall short and instead it's them God derides.
Thus I say God's judgement is fair, the proud
Toppled, the faithful with salvation endowed.

* A theme of Psalmists and Prophets that becomes the cup of salvation (Psalm 116) through Christ at Communion.

Psalm 116. The Cup of Judgement in Psalm 75 becomes the Cup of Salvation.

I'm pleased the Lord heard my prayer, therefore
I shall address Him always all my days.
I felt like death, as if drawn down to hell:
When so troubled I beseeched the Lord to quell
My anxiety for deliverance pays:
The Lord is gracious, we praise Him more.
He preserves the simple: when in misery
He helped me, He exercises mercy.
I will walk before Him 'mongst the living.
How can I reward the Lord's benefits?
I will receive the cup of salvation.
I'll speak publicly, avoid temptation;
Having freedom I'll serve Him as befits.
I'll offer Him sacrifices of thanksgiving.

Draw near with faith.

Today the Lord called me to dine
But where he is I've no idea.
You'll find me in the bread and wine.

He fed the twelve that would recline
Questioned by a friend held dear.
Today the Lord called me to dine.

You'll find me in the bread and wine.
Communion frees the soul from fear
Gathering community I call mine.

Today the Lord called me to dine
That I'll find him there is quite clear
The sacraments are what define.

You'll find me in the bread and wine
That still small voice is what I hear
Today the Lord called me to dine
You'll find me in the bread and wine.

www.ingramcontent.com/pod-product-compliance
Lightning Source LLC
LaVergne TN
LVHW051129080426
835510LV00018B/2308